Cat
purrsonality
test

Cat

purrsonality
test

Alison Davies

Illustrated by Alissa Levy

WHITE LION
PUBLISHING

Contents

Introduction

The feline psyche is complex. Beautiful, enigmatic, silly and sweet, there's nothing more contrary than a cat. A curiosity clothed in fur, our moggies lead us a merry dance and as long as it's to their tune they play ball. Just when you think you have your puss sussed, it turns things on their head and leaves you scratching yours. Hardly surprising, when you consider how domestic cats are commonly thought to have infiltrated the human world as early as *c.* 4400 BC.

In line with their trademark mystique, it's hard to pin down domesticated cats' exact origins and even harder to remember a time when they weren't a part of the family, warming our laps, knocking over our plants, inspecting boxes, stealing our hearts and perhaps even occasionally contemplating our demise.

The Egyptians believed cats were gods and treated them as such; a fact our felines have never forgotten. With this in mind, it can be hard for us lowly ones to read our kitties and to know what really makes them tick. This book is here to assist you and to give you an insight into your cat's true character. By looking at your moggy's behaviour in different settings, you'll get an idea of its personality type and that will help you to create a deeper bond.

Working out your cat is a lifelong process. You may never fully crack the kitty code, but you will have fun trying. Different breeds have their own traits, which gives us a head's up (see pages 122–25). Even so, don't be fooled by type. Cats are contradictory. There is no one-size-fits-all in cat country, which is where this book comes in.

Cats, like us, are utterly unique, and while they might fit into the carefully crafted categories outlined overleaf, this is not set in stone. Cats are full of surprises and often switch type, depending on internal and external circumstance. For example, the normally demure kitty might turn into a feral wild cat when faced with the dreaded flea and worming treatment, and the cat with swagger might lose his cattitude at the growl of the vacuum cleaner.

How To Use This Book

Each of the following nine chapters is a test comprising nine questions, geared towards a different area of a cat's life (all nine of them!). Simply pick the answers that most resonate with your puss, then add up the letters and discover which of the four cat profiles is a match.

    As you work through the tests, you'll recognize your kitty's quirks and the lovable things it does that makes it special. While you might find common ground in each quiz, you will also discover how multi-faceted your moggy is. If you don't end up with definitive answers, don't despair! Remember, cats are uniquely different to every other creature on the planet, and that includes us.

    While this book is based on scientific research, it is not a scientific book, rather a guide to help you understand your cat and its unique traits. At the end of the day, nobody knows your cat better than you, so enjoy, be entertained and know that whatever its personality type, your cat is purrfect as it is!

The Feline Five

There are thought to be five main personality traits seen in cats, known as the 'feline five' (see right). On every profile you'll discover which one, two or three of these traits best represents your cat, according to that area of their life. Add these up as you go, and keep score on page 118 to establish which character traits are most dominant in your cat overall.

The Feline Five Factors

2

EXTROVERSION

suggests an active and open mind, and points to a curious, inventive and fun-loving character.

3

DOMINANCE

indicates a puss who is assertive and aggressive.

1

NEUROTICISM

refers to anxiety issues and fearfulness, and denotes a shy, timid personality.

4

IMPULSIVENESS

signals an adventure seeker who is restless and reckless.

5

AGREEABLENESS

refers to a cat who displays affection easily and has a gentle and friendly personality.

Top Cat

How Are Your Cat's Confidence Levels?

Cats are solitary creatures but they can live together, whether in a multi-cat household or just rubbing along with the neighbours. Some positively thrive in company, while other more reserved kitties prefer to be the sole occupant and king or queen of all they survey. Lions have a hierarchical structure within their pride, and while our domestic beauties may not be as organized or sociable, they still have their tiers and fears when it comes to establishing the alpha cat.

It's not just other cats that need to watch out. As humans we are subject to dominant behaviour and can end up jumping to the tune of a pushy puss. You might think you're the boss, but don't be too sure. When it comes to the power of the paw, your cat might be using all of its kitty wiles to get its way, helpfully guiding you to the fridge and back with a bowl of fresh salmon without you even realizing how it happened.

Q1. How do you think your cat views you?

A As ma or pa.

B As a servant to his every whim.

C As a lowly human.

D His BFF (best feline friend) all the way.

Q2. Cats have been known to be fickle with their affections. Does your kitty spread the love, or is she a strictly one-person feline?

A You can confidently say you are the centre of her world.

B She switches favourites depending on who she needs to manipulate.

C This loose lady changes her feelings towards you as quickly as you change her litter tray.

D She's friendly with most people, but you're her favourite.

Q3. Whether you're a multi-cat household or not, your cat will come into contact with other felines. How does he react?

A He gives them a wide berth.

B He assesses the situation and keeps a wary distance.

C Mostly with verbal aggression and the threat of violence.

D He goes in for a sniff, and follows up with friendly 'chirrup'.

Q4. How would your cat assert her authority with you?

A She's too sweet for that.

B A gentle but persuasive bat of the paw.

C She grumbles and does an impression of 'grumpy cat'.

D You're always on the same page, so she never needs to.

Q5. In a fight for the best spot on the sofa, your cat ...

A Shares it with you.

B Showers you with love and slowly sidles in next to you.

C Jumps up, shoves his derriere in your face and forces you to shuffle over.

D Who needs the sofa when he can claim your lap?

Q6. Your cat wants to go out, you need to keep him in. How do you resolve this argument?

A She admits defeat and finds a suitable spot to snooze.

B She kills you with kindness, brushing in between your ankles until you release her.

C She stands by the door, wailing until you acquiesce.

D She's happy, as long as you entertain her with her favourite game of catch-the-mouse.

Q7. **How would your cat assert his authority when faced with an unknown human?**

A Being a timid kitty, he'd be gone before they stepped through the door.

B He plays nice one minute, then flexes his claws the next.

C He's highly vocal, and warns them from getting too close by hissing/growling at the top of his voice.

D He prefers to take a back seat and suss them out from a distance.

Q8. **Share and share alike. When it comes to food and other kitties from inside or outside the home, is your cat a hoarder or a generous girl?**

A She's happy to divvy up the snacks once she's taken her fair share.

B For this aloof feline, she's top table, top food, and served in her own bling bowl.

C There's a reason why the first two letters of 'mealtime' are 'me'. This puss doesn't do sharing. End of.

D Self-sufficient and resourceful, she doesn't care either way.

Q9. Your hungry kitty has taken a dislike to his usual food brand. What happens next?

A He turns up his nose for a minute, then gives in to the hunger pangs.

B He alternates between the fridge and curling in between your legs until you give him another option.

C He wails loudly at everything you put in front of him until he's satisfied with the choice.

D He politely miaows until you offer him something else.

The
Results

The Baby

NEUROTIC & AGREEABLE

This furry lovely may be large in more ways than one, but in her mind she's all kitten. A baby at heart, she looks to you in all things. More than likely an anxious puss, you are her security blanket and the first port of call when she feels nervous, which is most of the time. Loving and caring, she'll adore those one-to-one moments when she has you all to herself. In your arms, she feels like a blossoming flower in the summer sun. She is more than likely a house cat, but if she does go out she's unlikely to stray far from your apron strings. As far as the Baby is concerned, you are the top of the tree, and that's how she likes it. While most felines are supremely independent, she missed the memo. Luckily that's fine with you. As moggy mama, you are happy to nurture this beauty and give her the extra special care she craves.

Top Cat

The Godfather

EXTROVERTED & IMPULSIVE

Quick, slick and feline crafty, this puss is foxier than a furtive fox. He moves under the radar. Like a thief in the night, he'll steal your heart and your wallet, and you won't even care. Master manipulator, he knows that softly-softly goes a long way in the race to be Top Cat. Affection is currency, and he gets the most out of his money. Even so, he does adore you. He just loves you even more when you do what he wants. Pulling the strings with his human comes easy, but other cats are not so breezy. He'll avoid conflict because he doesn't need the stress, unless it's worth the catfight. He thinks it's better to bide his time, evaluating and planning world domination from your lap. Unpredictable and sometimes spontaneous, you can't rest on your laurels with the Godfather, but, let's face it, that's part of the reason you're partial to this puss.

Mostly

C

Top Cat

EXTROVERTED & DOMINANT

This noisy feline has no problem expressing herself. If she feels it, you feel it too. She likes to share the love – and her displeasure – in equal amounts. Humans are a necessary evil. It's not that she dislikes them entirely – you're tolerable in small doses – it's just that nothing matches her moggy magnificence. How could it? She's a superior being, from her finely tuned whiskers to the super luxe coat of fur that she leaves in copious amounts around the home, but she's not afraid to get down and dirty, particularly if an errant puss invades her space. Your tabby will never be an up close and personal kind of girl. For her, space is key and any cat in close proximity would do well to heed her warning glare. When she goes off, she's like a rocket. Aggressive, yes, but not with her human. She likes to dominate, and as long as you understand that she's boss, you'll have nothing to worry about!

Top Cat

20

Best Buddy

EXTROVERTED & AGREEABLE

Everyone's mate, this marvellous moggy has you at 'miaow'.
He'll always introduce himself and he likes to make new friends.
Easy to be around, there's nothing demanding about this puss.
He's a self-sufficient dude with a pleasant attitude. It takes a lot
to get him rattled. Power battles just aren't his thing. At the end
of the day, a comfy lap makes his heart sing and if it belongs to
his best bud, then even better. There's nothing he loves more
than hanging out with you. From reading fashion mags to rifling
through bags, he's an active kitty who
likes to share in your favourite things.
One of the gang, he doesn't want to
be top of the tree. Social climbing
is as bad as the real thing –
heavy on the paws and
claws. For him, true joy
is in being equals, two
compadres taking on
the world together!

Day-To-Day Kitty

What Are Your Cat's Daily Routines?

Cats, like humans, approach daily life in different ways. Some seek out adventure, while others prefer a quieter path. Usually fans of routine, most cats appreciate familiarity, whether it's a secure space to seek sanctuary or a specific time for food and grooming, but, as with all things, life can get in the way.

How your cat reacts to daily difficulties and interruptions gives you an insight into its deepest needs. As its owner, you'll know your cat's general mood and disposition, and you'll also know when and if this changes. Subtle shifts in personality reveal your feline's strengths and weaknesses. If you want to get closer to your moggy, look to the everyday things that you do together and how you can make its day more enjoyable. Pander to your puss's mercurial moods and go with the feline flow. Even if you're not into surprises, you might find you secretly enjoy your kitty's spontaneous streak!

Q1. Whether it's the daily commute to work or a trip to the supermarket, we all have to leave home at some point. For our cats this can be heaven or hell. How does your puss react?

A He feigns disinterest, and continues his claw manicure.

B He waits until you're almost out of the door then smothers you in a layer of cat hair.

C He weaves in between your feet in a game of 'trip you up'. If he maims you, you'll have to stay and play.

D He sits by the door looking sorry for himself until your return.

Q2. From unexpected visitors to family gatherings, the home can be a busy place for the average moggy. How does your cat feel about others intruding in her space?

A She takes the opportunity to strut the catwalk and share her exquisiteness with newcomers.

B Every visitor is a squidgy new lap-in-waiting.

C As long as they bring catnip toys, they're in!

D Cheesy biscuit treats secreted about the person are the only way for unknown humans to make friends.

Q3. The largest part of your cat's day is spent ...

A Making himself look feline fabulous! Groomed, polished, purrfection ...

B In the land of nod. Nap, chill, doze, repose.

C Playing, chasing, hunting, sniffing. Living every moment to the fullest.

D Having the munchies; if the mouth ain't moving, the kitty ain't grooving!

Q4. From easy-going to highly strung, you can usually read your kitty's mood from her expression. What's your cat's daily disposition like?

A Indifferent.

B Chilled.

C Curious.

D Loving.

Q5. It's the day most felines fear: the annual check-up with the vet. How does your puss react?

A Disdainful. How dare you disturb his daily beauty regime? The things he has to put up with!

B Relaxed. The journey is a great excuse to catch some Zzzz and to be with you.

C You'll have to catch him first.

D He cowers in the corner doing his best impression of a 'scaredy cat'.

Q6. **It's pill time, the words every owner dreads. What kind of patient is your cat?**

A A grumpy one, being force-fed a pill is not a pretty look.

B She allows you to feed her the pill, without any fuss.

C She's off! She knows something is up, and she's not hanging around to find out what.

D If it's disguised in a lump of cheese, then it's a breeze.

Q7. **Every feline has its safe place to retreat to when it all gets too much. Where does yours hole up when the going gets tough?**

A On his special fluffy cushion on top of the wardrobe.

B Snug and cosy, curled in the corner of the sofa.

C On the window ledge hidden behind the curtain, so he can make a quick exit.

D On top of the fridge freezer, out of reach and close to the primary food source.

Q8. **If you had to pinpoint a favourite moment/time of day with your kitty, it would be ...**

A Any moment when she shows a crumb of affection.

B Night-time, when you're chilling together on the sofa.

C Playtime takes the cat biscuit and gives you special time together.

D When you come home, and she runs to greet you in a flurry of fur.

Day-To-Day Kitty

Q9. **From emotional guzzlers to those who eat to live, your cat's relationship to food reveals a deeper side to its character. Which description most suits your moggy?**

A   He maintains the right to turn his nose up at any sub-standard offerings.

B   This cat trusts his gut. If he's feeling chipper, anything goes, but if he's under par, then his appetite goes.

C   This feline sees grub as fuel to feed the fire in his belly.

D   Food is life, simple as.

The Results

Cool Kitty
NEUROTIC & EXTROVERTED

Aloofness is what this puss is all about. In the hierarchy of cats and humans, she sits right at the top, looking down at her minions. While she's not overly dominant, her power is in 'disinterest'. She'll engage on her terms and it's up to you to follow suit. Her daily routine is important to her, but don't think she is a creature of habit. Far from it. If she fancies a change she'll let you know in no uncertain terms. While not openly extrovert, she is smart and in control. This girl likes to take the lead. Appearance is key and she must look her best at all times. Regular grooming sessions, where you do all the work, are essential. While she sets herself apart from other cats (and humans) she's a softy at heart and secretly adores attention. Treat her like a princess and you'll get the best back.

Day-To-Day Kitty

King of Chill
EXTROVERTED & AGREEABLE

This dude has zen sussed. He's happy in his own fur, confident and rocking the chill vibe. He doesn't need to dominate. You'll find no neurosis here! This kitty is calm and affectionate and responds to more of the same. He makes friends easily, and probably knows all the neighbours, having several patches to catch some rays. Come rain or shine, this cat's even temperament makes him the ideal snuggle buddy and cuddling up with you is his favourite thing to do. The noisy purring says it all! Likely to get on with other animals, cross species, he's not fussy; his open heart means he'll accept most things and people. Unfortunately, this also makes him a target in scuffs and skirmishes. He'll always see the best in his feline foes and will mostly avoid confrontation. After all, he's a lover not a fighter.

Day-To-Day Kitty

Artful Dodger

EXTROVERTED & IMPULSIVE

Quick, nimble, fast and flinty, this feline is a whirlwind of activity. Freedom is what makes her tick and her curious mind needs to be occupied. Whether she's joining you in a spot of morning yoga or investigating a crack on the wall, she needs to be busy. An extrovert at heart, she's brave, daring and up for almost anything – as long as it's her decision. Some of her favourite pastimes include moving objects around the house to ensure you get plenty of exercise searching for them, and playing with your feet. The eternal kitten, her impish nature provides plenty of Instagram pics, clips and anecdotes. Boredom will be a thing of the past with this kitty, as will any semblance of a sofa – she loves to scratch, sniff, tear and run riot. The key to her heart is in keeping her occupied. Engage her playful spirit and you'll have a friend for life.

Day-To-Day Kitty

Coy Cat

NEUROTIC & AGREEABLE

Sweet, shy and often retiring, this gorgeous boy might appear to be a loner, but he loves spending time with you. His anxiety means he doesn't fare well in large groups and can often feel intimidated by other cats and humans. Having said that, he can be swayed with plenty of patience and cat treats. His tummy is where it's at, and if you want to gain his trust, then food and sweet nothings is the way to go. Routine rules with this kitty, and any slight change could have him fleeing to his safe place, but once he's got over his initial nerves, he'll be ok, as long as you are with him every step of the way. Never aggressive or pushy, this introverted boy craves reassurance, so lots of cuddles, head-butts and quiet moments together are a must.

Day-To-Day Kitty

Moggy Mastermind

How Does Your Cat's Mind Work?

In folklore, felines rock a mystical vibe. Whether as witches' cohorts (or witches themselves, transformed into animal form), or fairy consorts, with eyes that are portals to the fey realm, *cats are magical*. They tingle with the supernatural, from the tips of their tails to the end of their whiskers.

They're super-talented too, gifted with supreme dexterity, agile limbs and the ability to balance in the most precarious of situations. Couple this with a quick-thinking brain, and you have the equivalent of an animal superhero. Just as humans have different strengths, so too do our cats. Yours might not be a genius but it could excel in street smarts and speed. Then again, you could be harbouring the equivalent of a kitty mastermind. Whatever gifts your cat holds dear, the fact your moggy can twist you around its paw with ease is proof enough of its prowess!

Q1. **Just like dogs, cats can take instruction if they really want to. How does your puss react when you ask her to do something?**

A   She gives you her best 'talk to the paw' expression.

B   The biscuit treat is all the motivation she needs.

C   She engages for a while, but an errant butterfly causes her to lose interest.

D   She stretches, yawns, then feigns sleep.

Q2. **You've left the house and accidentally shut your cat in the bedroom. What does your puss do?**

A   He leaves a toilet treat on your mattress, just so you know not to do it again.

B   He figures out how to open the door using his weight, the handle and some kitty dexterity.

C   He escapes through the slither of an open window.

D   He crawls under the duvet and waits for your return.

Q3. **Where does your cat poop?**

A   In the neighbour's garden, of course!

B   In the litter tray, and always neatly presented.

C   Outside, as nature intended.

D   Mostly in the litter tray, but she has been known to leave gifts around the home.

Moggy Mastermind

Q4. You've recently moved home. How long does it take your cat to feel comfortable and confident in his new pad?

A He instantly commandeers a spot and makes it known that this is 'his' safe place.

B He patrols each room, checking out every corner and cobweb for intruders.

C He finds his groove after the first day and settles with little fuss.

D He hides for at least a week, only coming out for food.

Q5. The TV is on and it's your favourite nature show. How engaged is your cat?

A She's more interested in curling up on your lap than what's on the box.

B Her ears prick up at the birds tweeting and she can't take her eyes off the screen.

C She's trying to catch the birds, pouncing, poking and stalking the TV.

D The shrill call of nature has her heading for the safety of her bed.

Q6. **It's a sunny day, but you know there's a storm brewing. How does your cat react?**

   A   He refuses to move from the sofa, despite the sunshine.

   B   He's restless, pacing in circles and looking out of the window.

   C   He doesn't care, he's an outdoor kitty.

   D   He comes running in at the first drop of rain to keep you company.

Q7. **When you come home from the shops your kitty is ...**

   A   Curled up in her favourite spot.

   B   At the window waiting for you.

   C   Out and about.

   D   Hiding in her safe place.

Q8. **We know that cats have a sixth sense, but what would your puss's psychic superpower be?**

   A   He's the Uri Geller of cats, able to read your mind and know what's best for you.

   B   His Sherlock Holmes sleuthing skills.

   C   His Houdini-style gift for escapology.

   D   Doing his best impression of the Invisible Man, especially when you have company.

Q9. When you call your puss by name, she ...

A Comes if it suits her, but if she's otherwise engaged, you can wait.

B Responds with a loud miaow to let you know she's heard.

C Is nowhere to be seen.

D Is already there, at your feet waiting for a cat treat.

The
Results

The Profiteer

EXTROVERTED & DOMINANT & IMPULSIVE

Meet the Machiavelli of moggies. This canny cat seems harmless on the surface, but don't be fooled. She knows exactly what she's doing. She will covertly suss out a situation while retaining an air of indifference. She balances dominance with openness and a slither of spontaneity, making her ready to seize the day and make the most of changing trends. While others might think outside the box or use all their kitty smarts to solve problems, this mastermind goes a step further and asks what she can gain from each turn of events. When presented with options, she goes for the one that serves her best. The Profiteer puss likes an easy life, and as long as she gets her way, she's happy!

Moggy Mastermind

The Genius

EXTROVERTED & IMPULSIVE & AGREEABLE

The genial Genius spends his days testing Newton's law of gravity, while wondering how to apply the theory of relativity to a stint of bird-catching. His active mind means he's always on the go, searching for new experiments and experiences. A people-pleaser, there's nothing he likes more than seeing his human smile, but while he's easy to train he won't always do what you want. This inquisitive boy needs stimulus and if it's not provided on the home front he'll venture further afield. He's likely to have a large territory because he loves to explore. He particularly loves self-assembly kits, where he can get his paws dirty and nose around the nuts and bolts of an object. A devoted lover of life, fun and you, he'll be sure to keep you entertained with his antics.

Moggy Mastermind

The Pragmatist

EXTROVERTED & DOMINANT & AGREEABLE

The Pragmatist has a built-in escape mechanism. Hard to pin down, she loses interest quickly and prefers the lure of the open road to the warmth of an open lap. That's not to say that she doesn't enjoy a cuddle, but it has to be on her terms. Being outside is important to her and she won't like being restricted in any way. Her IQ might not be at the top of the scale but she's smart and able to handle herself. Her skillset is more practical than philosophical, and she oozes confidence in the way she moves and navigates unchartered territory. If you're looking for a low-maintenance furry friend, this 'what you see is what you get' moggy fits the bill. Her straightforward approach to life is disarming and she's a joy to be around (when you can find her).

Moggy Mastermind

The Soft Touch

NEUROTIC & AGREEABLE

This guy may appear to be a scaredy cat – and it's true he's
nervous and jumps at the drop of a hat, literally – but he's
also deeply sensitive. While he might not have the street
smarts of other more bolshy feline specimens, he more than
makes up for it in his ability to read you. When you are sick
or feeling low, he's the first one on the scene. His love knows
no end and he'll smother you with affection, cat hair and a
plethora of purrs when you truly need it. His anxiety is deep-
rooted, but with the help of his human he'll learn to trust and
take things in his stride. Timid yet tactile, he's happy with
his lot. He doesn't need action or adventure; this home boy
takes comfort from familiar sights and sounds and learns at
his own purrfectly steady pace.

Moggy Mastermind

Puss-In-Boots

What Is Your Cat's Beauty Routine?

With so many beautiful breeds, it's hard not to love more than one. Cats know this and use it to their advantage. Some trade on cuteness while others are happy to do their own thing and be admired from afar.

But it's not all about vanity. Cats require a level of maintenance to help them look and feel their very best. Grooming boosts circulation, clears matted fur and also provides human and cat bonding time. While the prissy puss may love the fuss, others prefer to let Mother Nature take over. Fashion savvy felines take the haute couture route and positively thrive with lots of attention, while those more introverted stay under the radar, and under the hedge.

Beauty is in the eye of the beholder, but the look your cat rocks says a lot about its confidence and how it interacts with others, and the general level of maintenance it prefers speaks volumes about its personality.

Q1. **Your cat would describe her daily beauty regime as ...**

A Non-existent. Who gives a whiskers what I look like when there are adventures to be had.

B Not a hair out of place, darrrrling.

C As nature intended. I am beautiful as I am.

D Hit and miss, from rockin' the Wild Cat to going full on Puss Couture, I mix it up.

Q2. **It's Christmas and you've gone all out with the glitzy decorations, but how does your cat feel about a festive tweak or two?**

A Baubles and tinsel – not for wearing but great for chasing!

B Sparkles, glitter and a sweet smelling shampoo. What's not to love?

C If he wanted to be a Christmas tree he'd sprout branches.

D Yes to a festive bow, no to the frumpy Santa hat.

Q3. It's time to prep your puss for her photo shoot, but how does she feel about throwing a pose?

A Catatonic.

B Charismatic.

C She couldn't care less.

D Curious.

Q4. You and your kitty are in full snuggle mode. What does your cat smell like up close and personal?

A Damp soil and dustbins.

B He loves an expensive cologne.

C Home.

D Your favourite sweet treat.

Q5. When your cat's in the mood, how does she like to be stroked?

A She lets you know by positioning the relevant body part in front of you for attention.

B She'll play passive, as long as she gets a full-on body massage.

C A quick head rub is this girl's preferred mode of stroke.

D Tickling is where it's at, from under the chin to along the belly, this lady loves to wriggle!

Q6. It's party central at your home, and you have a full house of friends and family. Your puss sees this as the purrfect opportunity to ...

A Chase the birds in the garden.

B Show off his magnificence and build a bigger fan base.

C Do his own thing while you're occupied.

D Cause a stir by stealing nibbles and jumping on laps.

Q7. Good table manners speak volumes, but is your cat a classy date or a messy moggy at mealtimes?

A Face hits bowl every time, fully submerged, nose, whiskers and all.

B Each mouthful is chewed and savoured in style.

C Being a grazer means this puss dips in and deposits snacks around the house.

D This no-rush kitty sometimes uses a paw to scoop out those hard to reach morsels.

Q8. What would your cat's hashtag be?

A #Cattitude.

B #FelineFatale.

C #CuddleCat.

D #Puss-in-boots.

Q9. When it comes to her safety quick release collar, what style do you think your cat prefers?

A Plain simple, without frills, fuss and bells!

B A classy pink affair, with a bit of sparkle.

C She's a bare-necked lady, and proud!

D This girl rocks a silver studded collar.

The
Results

The Boss

DOMINANT & AGREEABLE

A cat is a cat and that is that. This puss has no illusions. He doesn't have to pretend to be anything else. He doesn't care. Life is for living, and when there's a bird to chase and grass to graze on, there's no time for plumping and preening. A free spirit at heart, this kitty embraces every aspect of his feline nature. He knows that no-one does CAT better than he can. An adept hunter, he uses all his senses and skills to be the best version of himself. His confident nature means he's probably a popular character in the neighbourhood. Making his presence felt in whatever way he can, he'll use his wily nature to get your attention. He loves a fuss as much as the next cat, but it has to be on his terms. A leader not a follower, he'll happily stay by your side and share the journey (as long you can take direction).

Puss-In-Boots

The Fashionista

EXTROVERTED & DOMINANT

This gorgeous girl has got it all going on. A feline trend-setter, she's not afraid to venture where other cats fear to tread. Anything to build her fan base! Quirky and original, she's an extrovert and a total flirt. She might appear fickle in her fancies, but it's all about feeling the love. For her, attention is key. The more she has, the happier she'll be, so be prepared to share her with friends, family and anyone who enters your domain. While she's not averse to playing dress-up, don't overdo it. Even she has her limits. Dedication is what she demands. If you're willing to put in the time and effort, pamper with a passion and groom, groom, groom, she'll reward you with her best star pose.

Puss-In-Boots

The Bare-Faced Beauty

EXTROVERTED & AGREEABLE

This boy's charm is in his ability to be himself. He doesn't need to try; he's a natural beauty. He is easy on the eye and in the arms. With plenty to grab hold of, he's a cuddle in furry form. Naturally, being such a carefree kitty he has many admirers but the secret to his success is simple: he's happy with what he's got. Outgoing and affectionate, making friends comes easily to him, but while his affability shines through, he's no walkover (and definitely no walk in the park kitty on a lead). Make him look ridiculous and the purr will become the grrrrrrr. Treat him with respect and you'll tame the tiger within. He likes a free rein and his own territory but he's a home boy at heart – where you are will always be his safe place.

Puss-In-Boots

The Icon

DOMINANT & IMPULSIVE

Meet the real Puss-in-Boots, over-the-knee leather of course!
She's the Monroe of moggies, and all KITTY; jaunty, edgy and
ready to mix it up. This lady puts the purr in powerful. She's
spontaneous, impulsive and almost always not what you expect.
Bite the hand that feeds – she just might, but it could all change
in a heartbeat. Get her over-excited and you'll pay the price.
Better to let her be. This is what she does best. If you're looking
for character, this beauty has it by the bucket-load. She'll
entertain your friends, win your heart with her affectionate ways
and curl up on your most expensive chiffon scarf, just because
she can. There's no reason to her rhyme, but that's what makes
her so unforgettable.

Puss-In-Boots

Paws, Snooze, Repeat

What Are Your Cat's Sleeping Patterns?

There's nothing more peaceful than the sight of a sleeping cat – cute, calm and oozing Zen. Our moggies are masters of the snooze. They know the importance of grabbing some Zzzz and allowing time to let body and mind recharge; a lesson we could learn too. It may seem like they're always asleep, but just like humans this varies and falls somewhere between twelve and sixteen hours a day. Even so, sleeping does take up a big chunk of their life, so it's essential they get it right.

The wrong dozing spot can turn a happy cat into a snappy cat, and once they're curled up and comfy it's about the wriggle room as well. Like humans, they enter a REM sleep state, which means they also dream – although about what is anyone's guess. Your cat's bedtime habits reveal what's important to kitty, and how in control it likes to be. Every puss knows that getting plenty of rest is the key to kitty well-being.

Q1. It can be tricky sharing a bed or sofa with your furry friend, especially if it's the preferred place for a power nap. Where is your cat's favourite snoozing spot?

A Anywhere you happen to be, taking up your space in bed or snuggling close, can't tell which!

B Anywhere he happens to be: sock drawer, magazine rack, bathroom basin ... preferring a snug, confined space, he'll often take it over and spread into it.

C Anywhere he shouldn't be: next door, three streets down with the kitties about town.

D In his fleecy igloo, with the special 'Top Cat' insignia: why would he be anywhere else?

Q2. Some cats are routine queens, while others run riot when it comes to anything regular. How does your kitty behave at bedtime?

A Quick to bed, early to rise and rally the troops for breakfast (meaning you).

B A game of hide-and-seek is a must before retiring for the evening.

C Bedtime? What's that?

D It's lights out, on the dot, not a minute too soon, not a minute past and should you dare to deviate, she'll unleash the diva!

Q3. **Like humans, cats have dreams and sometimes nightmares, so what does your kitty dream of as he slips into the land of nod?**

A Did someone mention sl— Zzzzzzz …

B One cardboard box, two cardboard box, three cardboard box.

C Forget chasing the dragon, you can't beat chasing the butterfly!

D Delicate slithers of thinly sliced smoked salmon on a bed of juicy plump prawns …

Q4. **Sleeping positions speak volumes about how we feel, but when your cat assumes the position, she likes to …**

A Stretch on her back, legs akimbo, tongue out … Pure joy!

B Make like a wriggly worm and fit into every crevice.

C Chill on the spot, one eye open and ready for action.

D Curl neatly into a ball, tail wrapped snugly around body. Kitty perfection.

Q5. **Who is your kitty's snuggle buddy?**

A You of course!

B His favourite toy or furry friend.

C The sun is his bedfellow.

D He likes his bed all to himself.

Q6. From sleepwalking to snoring, we're an active bunch during slumber, and our cats are in on the act too! What does your feline do when she's asleep that really takes the 'cat' biscuit?

A Snore.

B Fidget.

C Stare.

D Pose.

Q7. Most moggies emit an air of Zen when they are sleeping. If yours could talk, what sleep advice would he give you?

A Don't think about it, just do it.

B Move more, snooze more.

C Who needs sleep?

D Doesn't matter how you do it, just make sure it's in Egyptian cotton sheets!

Q8. When your cat is asleep by your side or on your lap she makes you feel...

A Sleepy.

B Happy.

C Suspicious.

D Privileged.

Q9. What type of self-care would your cat practise to help him relax?

A He'd be a master at meditation and breathing.

B Mindfulness helps him engage with his surroundings and live for right now!

C Hot yoga gives this action man his moves.

D A kitty massage makes him look and feel his best.

The Results

The Dude

AGREEABLE

If this cat could talk, his phrase of choice would be 'chill out guys'. While chaos is all around, the Dude channels Zen. That's not to say that he doesn't get excited, but it's usually when his belly says so. Hunger is the only thing that gets him fired up. Once the tummy beast is satiated, kitty is calm and ready for his favourite pastime: a nap. If that impromptu snooze involves a snuggly human mattress, all the better! To be fair, this cat does have a tendency to think he's human. If he had his way, the bed would be *all* his, but he realizes that it's only fair to offer you a slither. After all, you make a good pillow most of the time. Exercise is most definitely out for this puss unless it's a spot of feline yoga, his top move being the 'roll, stretch, yawn' sleep salutation.

Paws, Snooze, Repeat

The Chameleon

EXTROVERTED

This hard-to-pin-down puss is a slippery character. There's strength in flexibility and this girl's elastic! Whatever the space, she'll find a way to inhabit it, just as she inhabits her own skin with ease. There's an inner confidence to the Chameleon, and if she sets her sights on something, she'll usually get it. But don't mistake her for wilful. Her curious nature means she'll want to investigate everything, from the inside of your Wellington boots to the inner sanctum of the fridge. The world is like a giant tin of sardines: slippery, smelly and inviting! That said, she also enjoys company. She'd like nothing more than to lead you on an adventure – whether that's down the garden path or behind the kitchen cupboards, she'll find a way to share the fun. And if you run out of games to play, there really is nothing more inviting than a cardboard box.

The Tearaway

IMPULSIVE

Who doesn't love a bad boy (or girl)? This top cat knows that a little feral attitude will take him far. That's not to say that he's naughty through and through, far from it. He just likes to exercise his right to party. All night if he can! 'Work hard, play hard' is his motto, and that means he's always on the lookout for fun, trouble and anything that will lead him off the beaten track. While he might not be a home bird, he appreciates a solid base, a pad from which he can venture out and return to, should he need a duvet day. This boy knows which side his bread is buttered, but he also enjoys his freedom. Don't try and rein him in, instead respect his roaming ways and be happy in the knowledge that it's you to whom he chooses to come home.

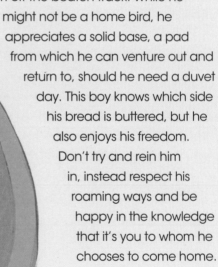

The Poser

DOMINANT

It's all about appearance for this prim puss. Slovenly doesn't do it, *at all*. She expects the best because she *is* simply the best. You'll rarely find a hair out of place or a shabby collar, but that doesn't mean it's all about the bling. In her case it's quality that counts. Own-brand cat food, no sirree! This magnificent example of moggydom likes top of the range, from the way she sleeps to her mattress of choice and the pouts she pulls. Speaking of which, you'll know if she's not entirely satisfied, by the look of disappointment, *in you*. Poser kitties think they're above everyone, so should anyone – cat or human – intrude upon her precious 'me time' they'll receive short shrift, and a paw in the face.

Paws, Snooze, Repeat

Purr
Time

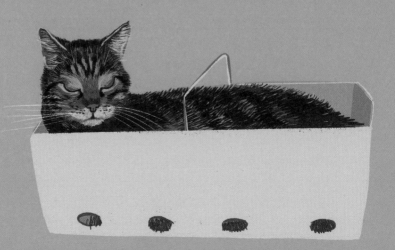

How Does Your Cat Like to Play?

While it's true that cats have got snoozing down to a fine art, they also love to play. It's an integral part of their development, helping them to hone primal instincts and improve hunting skills. Frolicking with frivolity also stimulates body and mind and keeps your furry friend at its feline finest. As your cat gets older, a regular dose of fun and games is essential exercise, assisting mobility and also strengthening the bones and the bonds between you. It's a stress reliever too!

While some cats are more enthusiastic than others, the way yours engages reveals a different side to their nature. Are they the life and soul of the party or a wimpy wallflower? A creative genius or the playground bully? You may find your cat falls into more than one category, depending on their mood, the situation and a number of other factors. Even if your moggy is lacking in merriment, don't give up. Play can transform a timid tabby into a tigress, all it takes is the right toys and games, and a little patience.

Q1. **You've got your friends around for a catch up, but kitty wants in. What's he likely to do?**

A   Assess the situation with a tentative sniff of each person's hand.

B   Hiss and show his teeth so they know who's boss.

C   Head-butt each new human until one decides to play with him.

D   Saunter across the room to show his displeasure at the intrusion.

Q2. **What game does your cat like playing with you?**

A   She likes to stalk the room, casing out every corner for possible intruders.

B   Attack the hand. She starts with gentle nudging, lulling your hand into a false sense of security, before launching full-on tooth and claw attack.

C   Tickle the tum. Bliss for owner and kitty alike.

D   The one where you try and convince your cat to play, and then count the seconds before she saunters off in the opposite direction.

Q3. When it comes to a cat collective, does your puss share the fun with other felines, or prefer to go solo?

A This boy likes to go it alone.

B He'll play along while it suits, but be warned, kitty's got claws!

C From sniffing butts to a rough and tumble wrestling match, he's up for anything.

D Given his superior status, he prefers to watch the madness from a distance.

Q4. As a treat, you've planted some catmint in the garden. What does your kitty do?

A She eyes it suspiciously, before going in for sniff.

B She launches herself full throttle into the leaves.

C She rolls in it until she's smothered in the green stuff.

D She looks from you to the plant and then back again, as if to say 'so'?

Q5. To your cat, a scrunched-up ball of foil is ...

A An alien being from another planet.

B A missile to be chased.

C A shooting star at which to marvel.

D A scrunched-up ball of foil.

Q6. **A fly has mistaken your living room for a safe spider-free zone. Your cat sees this as an opportunity to ...**

A Run up and down the room trailing its movements.

B Go in for the kill.

C Tap and tease the fly in a game of 'tag'.

D Watch you running around like a lunatic, trying to get it out of the window.

Q7. **Toys come in all shapes and sizes. What's your cat's favourite?**

A A chewed up, smelly woollen mouse he's had for years.

B A slipper he's mauled to bits.

C From carrier bags to golf balls, it's all got play potential.

D A snuggly catnip pillow.

Q8. **Your online delivery has arrived, leaving you with an empty cardboard box. Luckily, your cat's on hand to ...**

A Climb inside and guard the box from thieves.

B Use it as a scratching post and rip it to shreds.

C Have an impromptu game of 'in the box, out the box'.

D Turn it upside down and use it as a bunker.

Purr Time

Q9. You've bought a new toy: a felt mouse dangling on the end of a long stick. What does your cat make of it?

A 'Imposter! Get it away from me!'

B Hunting practice.

C 'Woo Hoo', play heaven!

D 'Really?! Seriously?! You want me to play with that thing?'

The
Results

The Spy

NEUROTIC & AGREEABLE

He'll never admit to being neurotic but this kitty does tend to think the worst. Cautious in demeanour, he takes a 'guilty until proven innocent' approach when it comes to new things. From toys, furnishings and fellow felines, it's all the subject of mistrust, but that doesn't mean he won't come around in the end. He needs time to get used to things, and that means some serious inspection and detection work. This terrific tabby is pure 007, putting surveillance at the top of his list. Once he's given a thorough assessment of the situation, and with time and encouragement, he'll be more accepting. He might not seem the most playful puss but his inner kitten will emerge when he's sure the coast is clear. Interactive games that involve just the two of you are the cat's whiskers. Reward his trust with a hefty dose of snuggles and watch his fun side surface.

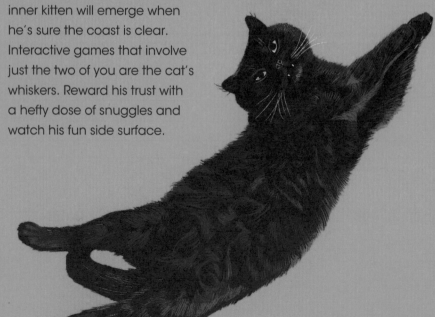

The Assassin

DOMINANT & IMPULSIVE

The Assassin is a masterful hunting machine. From snaffling fingers and toes to feathers and fur, she's not fussy, as long as there's a 'catch' at the end of it. Aggressive when pushed, she walks a fine line, and not just when she's balancing on the neighbour's fence. It doesn't take much to get her fired up, and like any sassy lady she loves the thrill of the chase. Play is energetic, frantic and feisty, a way to hone her skills for the real deal. Don't be surprised to find a trail of debris from her kills. Half-eaten insects will be her 'go-to' practice until she's ready for bigger game. That's not to say that she doesn't have a softer underbelly, although you'll certainly see no wobbly bits!

The key to playtime is to engage lightly. No excessive petting or fast moves to get her over-excited. Treat her with respect and she'll love you fiercely.

The Maverick

EXTROVERTED & AGREEABLE

Finding fun is what this feline does best. He'll sniff out the action by sticking his nose into any available crevice and, if there's no joy, he's the boy to make it happen! You might call him a party animal, but he's not just there for the japes. He likes to learn things. His curiosity must always be roused, for a 'piqued puss' is a picture of pleasure. Resourceful and able to amuse himself, he likes making new friends. Whether human or feline, a whiff of their scent is enough to assure him they'll be pals for life, but if not, he won't lose precious Zzzz over it. Luckily, the Maverick is easy to entertain. Give him room to run and roam and watch him roll. He'll always find his way home because that's where he has the most fun. Need a pick-me-up? Give him a ball of string and watch him go!

Purr Time

The Critic

DOMINANT & AGREEABLE

While some might say this tabby is condescending, she's really just a discerning soul. She knows what she likes, what she thinks and what she wants, and she'll let you know with delicate firmness. A gentle paw on the hand to say 'no', or a tush in the face is a negative meant with grace. She'll make her feelings obvious with little effort. A withering look from this puss would turn most mortals (and moggies) to stone, but you know her better than most and can read her moods. That's not to say that she isn't pleasure-seeking, she just prefers her fun to be a little more sedate. Catnip pillows and toys are the way to go with this luscious lovely. She'll luxuriate in their soft sweetness, allowing her to relax in a ladylike manner while others do all the rough and tumble. Why work hard when you can let the party come to you?

Purr Time

Cattitude

What Quirks Make Your Cat Unique?

Cats have attitude. From the tips of their pointy ears to the jaunty flick of a puffed-up tail, there's a wiggle in the walk and a swagger in the stalk. Everything they do has purpose; even snoozing is done in effortless style. Eccentric is the cat-phrase for those in the know. Who wants to be normal anyway? A pertinent puss knows there's power in the slightly perverse. As owners around the world can attest, cats make their mark in more ways than one. Yes, there'll be scratches on the arms and legs, but the pawprints in the heart are etched even deeper.

Your cat's idiosyncrasies are what transforms them into a miaowing masterpiece. This quiz examines your cat's individual quirks and what makes them stand out from the crowd. Each little difference adds to their purrsonality, because every puss is unique. The little things they do shows what really makes them tick.

Q1. Your cat wants to play. How does she let you know?

A She brings the party to you by jumping on your lap, dancing between your legs and running rings around you.

B She gets her favourite squidgy mouse and drops it at your feet.

C She lays resplendent at your feet, as if to say, 'I'm ready, entertain me'.

D She has a mad ten minutes, chasing her own tail and playing 'catch me' with an invisible assailant.

Q2. It's New Year's Eve and the neighbours are having a firework display. How does your cat react?

A He presses his face up against the window to get a good view.

B He's not impressed, but stays the other side of the curtain to keep guard.

C He hides and gets as far away from the chaos as possible.

D He sits on or near you. As long as you're close by, he knows he's safe.

Q3. What does your cat do to make you laugh out loud?

A Sleeps in the bathroom basin.

B Tries in vain to scale the curtains/blinds.

C Sits at the table, like a human.

D Chats away to you.

Q4. You've cooked your favourite spaghetti bolognese, but it also happens to be your cat's meal of choice. What happens next?

A You and he either end of a spaghetti string, re-enacting the scene from *Lady and the Tramp*.

B He sits by your plate and gazes intently at your mouth until you give in.

C First he sniffs, then if it's good enough he miaows loudly for service.

D He swipes a strand of spaghetti when you're not looking and carries it away to enjoy.

Q5. Most cats have weird eating habits. What's the strangest thing your cat has scoffed in her quest for a full tum?

A Curry. *Lots* of curry.

B A dragonfly, headfirst.

C Asparagus tips.

D Swiping a crust of bread left for the birds.

Q6. What really freaks out your cat?

A   Cucumbers.

B   You singing.

C   The vacuum cleaner.

D   Thunder and lightning.

Q7. If you could assign your cat a job in the human world, it would be ...

A   Box inspector: she likes to check them out in case they're harbouring fugitives or foreign objects.

B   Security guard: she's in charge of puss patrol and keeps the neighbourhood in check.

C   Food tester: she likes to sniff and taste your food to check for quality and potential poisoning.

D   Secret shopper: she's always bringing you odd gifts.

Q8. You're going in for a squeeze. How does your cat react?

A   He wraps his paws around you and gives you the full wet nose treatment.

B   He licks your face vigorously until you put him down.

C   He allows you a quick cuddle then wriggles his way out of it.

D   He adopts the prime snuggle pose and slips his head under your chin.

Cattitude

Q9. You've fired up the laptop to work. What's your cat up to?

A   Pawing at your fingers as you type. It's her new favourite game!

B   She sits patiently at your side, waiting for you to notice her.

C   Your keyboard is her new cat bed, and she refuses to move.

D   She chatters away as you work.

The
Results

A

The Screwball

DOMINANT & IMPULSIVE

This zany puss puts the 'P' into panache. She's winning at life every day in her own unique and quirky way. Anything goes with this kitty, so expect the unexpected ... and then some. This lady switches moods and tastes quicker than she changes cat food brands – and that's something she does a lot, but you don't mind. The extra effort is worth the entertainment you get from watching her antics. Want to make her day? Switch things up on the home front by moving a few things around. Give her something new to explore, and she'll find a million and one ways to play. After all, a shoe is not simply footwear, it's a highly complex vessel used to hone the art of squeezing into and out of places, thus improving overall elasticity, and strength of will!

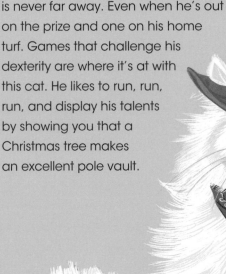

The Sheriff

EXTROVERTED & AGREEABLE

This boy is strong, agile and on the ball. He has a look that says, 'I dare you', which he especially reserves for feral felines that step out of line. If you need him, he's by your side in a heartbeat. When you're feeling down, he'll lift you up. His presence is calming, for while he might seem like your average cat, he's more dog than cat: loyal, loving and confident. His quirks are governed by his need to protect his own, and that means you and yours. Most likely to come when you call, this moggy-doggy is never far away. Even when he's out of sight, he's got one eye on the prize and one on his home turf. Games that challenge his dexterity are where it's at with this cat. He likes to run, run, run, and display his talents by showing you that a Christmas tree makes an excellent pole vault.

Cattitude

The Connoisseur

NEUROTIC & DOMINANT

There's class in the elegant swagger of this cat. The way she moves commands attention and a smile, and you can't help but marvel at her abundant curves as they take centre stage in your world. A diva? Perhaps, but it's more about quality and having the best of everything. She'll amuse you with her 'I am not amused' expression. The more stand-offish she becomes, the more you'll long for a cuddle, and she'll let you because deep down she knows the key to getting her heart's desire lies in making you happy. The Connoisseur takes herself seriously. Whether quaffing feline friendly *Cate*rnet Sauvignon or soaking up Vivaldi's *Four Seasons*, she does everything with finesse and, while she might not mean to be funny, her entitled nature will have you chortling morning to night. Let this precious puss have her moment in the sun and she's sure to throw some light your way.

Cattitude

The Comedian
EXTROVERTED & IMPULSIVE

This cat's sixth sense is his humour. It's as if he understands the slightest nuance in your voice and mimics it moggy style. A natural chatterbox, this sociable kitty is fast and nimble. Whether swiping a burger from the barbeque or fleeing capture for the cat carrier, he's no easy target. He could be sneaking ninja-like into next door for second breakfast or tap dancing in an open tin of paint, but one thing is for certain, he's up to no good. That said, this stand-up comedian specializes in improv, making each moment memorable. If you're looking for fun, you've found the one to make it happen. When this cat's around, everything is good game, including your toes, the remote control and your chicken noodle supper. With this chipper chap, it's all about having a laugh, and if it makes you laugh too, then that's an added bonus.

Cattitude

Chat With The Cat

How Does Your Cat Communicate?

The language of the cat is a mystical minefield to navigate, no surprise when you consider that your average feline has at least one hundred vocalizations to draw upon, and that's before we get to the confusing body language. But what, if anything, are cats trying to tell you and what does this say about their character?

Just like humans, some cats are introverted while others like to take centre stage. You might think your cat is indifferent, but do not be fooled. Research shows that cats understand a lot more than we think, and while they might play deaf when you call them in for tea, they recognize the sound of their name and know when they're being summoned. Whether they respond or not is up to them!

Q1. **To get your attention when it's 'second breakfast' time, your cat will ...**

A Unleash the claws and go in for the kill on the nearest surface, be it sofa, wall or Persian rug.

B Pull the cute card with a squeak and head-butt combo to the lower leg.

C Sit by the fridge and wail like a banshee.

D Give you a good talking to with a series of miaows and mewls rising in pitch to match the urgency of the situation.

Q2. **It may be your work space, but the cat got there first and he's not about to share. How does he let you know?**

A A grumble followed by the hint of a hiss keeps you in your place.

B The power of the purr never fails to lull you into a stupor.

C A furry bottom in the face always works.

D A raised eyebrow, then a firm paw and a face full of cattitude.

Q3. **Each cat has a unique way of showing that she cares. Your cat tells you she loves you by ...**

    A   A tummy tickle of course! Followed by a game of 'attack the hand'.

    B   Attaching a wet nose to your arm/leg, for a damp nuzzle and kiss.

    C   Offering stress relief in the form of some kneading. Kitty massage anyone?

    D   Coating you in her scent and a thick layer of cat hair, just in case you should get cold.

Q4. **You know when your cat isn't well, because he ...**

    A   Withdraws quietly from everything.

    B   Goes off his food and doesn't want to play.

    C   Gets more affectionate and wants to be near you.

    D   Tries to get your attention with faint cries.

Q5. **From the roar of the vacuum cleaner to your fluffy unicorn slippers, some things just set your puss off, but when she's really fired up she ...**

    A   Channels her inner tiger and grrrrrrrowls.

    B   Squeals and bolts for the nearest hidey hole.

    C   Fixes you with a stern 'How dare you!' stare.

    D   Flicks her tail in the air and stalks off in a huff.

Q6. There's nothing like a conversation with your cat at the end of a long day. When you talk to yours, he always ...

A Looks at you like you've lost the plot.

B Squeaks back at you; he might not understand but he's with you in spirit.

C Blinks, yawns then pretends to be asleep.

D Has a full-on conversation made up of chirps, squeals and chunters, leaving space for you to answer.

Q7. Canny cats never give the game away, they hide their guilt behind a blank expression, but for some felines it's all about the visage. What face does your cat like to pull?

A The kung fu battle face. Always.

B The butter wouldn't melt, super cute puss look.

C The gaze of one who is not amused.

D The 'Listen up, I shall say this only once' face.

Q8. You know when your cat has got the cream, because he will ...

A Allow a quick stroke.

B Purr deeply.

C Head-butt you several times.

D Mewl with delight and rub against your legs.

Q9. **From play to prey, when cats first meet it can be war or peace. How does your cat greet another?**

   A   With a puffed-up tail and a threatening hiss.

   B   First she'll go in for a gentle sniff.

   C   She might allow them to walk in her shadow if they're respectful.

   D   Excited squeaks and mewls are her way of saying 'hello' to a new friend.

The Results

The Warrior

DOMINANT & IMPULSIVE

It's not about what you say but what you *do* with this kitty. Actions speak louder than purrs, so why waste time with conversation when a swipe of the paw has the desired effect? What this confident cat lacks in vocal charm, she more than makes up for in presence. Don't underestimate her powers of persuasion though. As the old adage goes, 'Kitty's got claws and she's not afraid to use them!' She's Dominant with a capital D, and a little bit Diva too. Having said that, she's a softy at heart and can be tamed with a generous amount of love, roast chicken and catnip. Play is important to this feline and helps to keep the channels of communication open. Keep her busy and entertained and she'll return the favour by at least pretending to listen.

Chat With The Cat

The Charmer

NEUROTIC & EXTROVERTED

This kitty knows how to kill with kindness. A carefully placed paw, a soothing purr and a delicate squeak are the tools of his trade. It's true that the cat gods of old created the miaow purely for the benefit of gullible humans, knowing it would be enough to have them tearing open the nearest sachet of cat food in an instant, and this feline is a master at mind control. Not a fan of aggressive tactics, he'll flee at the first sign of a fight, but that doesn't mean he's faint-hearted. Patience and a bit of cheeky charm are enough to ensure that he always gets the cream. He's happy to let other cats (and you) take the lead. It's worth it to avoid an argument. Reward him with cuddles and kisses, and he'll have you smiling like the Cheshire Cat.

Chat With The Cat

C

The Royal Highness

NEUROTIC & DOMINANT

If you feel you're of royal blood like this posh puss, then there's really no need to dabble with waifs and strays. Her beautiful furry torso was put upon this earth for one thing only: to be adored. Communication is an effort for a cat of this calibre. She prefers to get her message across subliminally, believing that the power of her presence is enough to shake things up. Expressive but not overly emotional, unless her favourite cat treats are involved, she likes to get her own way. After all, it's all about her, and should you forget that she will remind you by throwing a tantrum of mammoth moggy proportions. It's impossible to win when it comes to human vs cat, but secretly you don't mind. Her outlandish behaviour makes you love her even more.

The Intellectual

EXTROVERTED & AGREEABLE

Communication is an art form for this philosophical puss, and unlike his feline friends he uses the full gamut of kitty sounds and vocalizations to get his point across. Adept at body language, he's not afraid to explore the finer nuances of his craft, using everything from the tips of his whiskers to the end of his tail to connect with you. While it's true that humans have a long way to go before they catch up with his superior intellect, this pussy is prepared to give them a chance, and he's more than happy to share some of his worldly expertise and experiences. He knows how you speak and will even mimic your tone to help you get the gist of the conversation. His only frustration comes from the fact that while humans pretend to listen, they rarely hear or understand the simplest of things or recognize that every other sentence ends with the word 'tuna'!

Chat With The Cat

Moggy On The Move

How Big is Your Cat's Sense of Adventure?

Territory matters. While outdoor cats may cover a vast terrain or simply covet next door's back yard, indoor cats get territorial too, especially when it comes to their home and owners. After all, our felines are wild at heart. Their natural instincts to run, hunt and defend their patch will always come to the fore. Even the coyest of kitties will find their roar when faced with an interloper. Male cats are usually more dominant, preferring their own space to patrol and protect, while female cats often overlap territories with less tension. Even so, urine spraying and fighting to the fur are common occurrences when our moggies meet on shared turf.

The territory your cat commands speaks volumes when it comes to confidence and spontaneity. Clingy kitties may be anxious, but the urge to protect their property – aka you – will also fuel their need. Whatever drives your feline forwards, their wandering ways (or not) are an important part of their kitty make-up.

Q1. Does your kitty share the love or is she strictly a one-person puss?

A She knows which side her bread is buttered, and home is where it's at.

B Other humans are alright; she doesn't mind sharing her affections as and when.

C As far as you know, she's got at least two other pads in the neighbourhood.

D In her world, there are just the four walls of her castle, and you're ok too!

Q2. If your cat was an action hero, who would he most resemble?

A The Hulk: sweet most of the time, but don't make him angry.

B James Bond: this kitty is super-fast, swish and parties hard.

C Indiana Jones: but that archaeologist has nothing on this cat's wandering ways.

D Batman: deeply private and mysterious, he likes his 'cat cave'.

Q3. **When the sun comes down and the night owls emerge, your tabby can be found ...**

A Snuggled on the sofa with you.

B Prowling outside, playing security guard.

C Living it up with the alley cats.

D Fed, watered and ready for bed.

Q4. **Around the neighbourhood your kitty is known as ...**

A The cute cat from number ...

B The kitty that likes to poop in our garden!

C The Lone Ranger, always out and about and up to mischief.

D What cat? Didn't know you had a cat!

Q5. **Another cat has wandered into your garden/outdoor space. What's the likely outcome?**

A Your puss will see him off, whatever it takes.

B A stand-off, with some hissing and tail puffing, but no major scuffle. Both sides retreat to a distance.

C It's unlikely she'll be there to notice!

D She's happily oblivious; her indoor realm is safe and secure and that's what matters.

Q6. It's a scorching hot day. Where are you likely to find your kitty?

A Beneath a bush in the shade.

B Lazing in the sunshine next door.

C You have no idea; he'll show up when he's hungry.

D On, near or in the fridge.

Q7. Has your cat ever gone AWOL for any length of time?

A No, you can set your watch by this routine-loving feline.

B There have been one or two hairy moments, but she always comes home eventually.

C This freedom-loving feline can be gone for days at a time. You no longer worry.

D She's good at finding hidey-holes inside, but a whiff of roast chicken does the trick.

Q8. When you let your cat out, he tends to....

A Stay close to home, mooching in the back yard/garden.

B Launch himself like a rocket over the fence and into the big wide world.

C He's out all the time anyway!

D He's an indoor kitty all the way.

Q9. Should your feline take to wandering, what would bring her home?

A   Your voice would be enough.

B   You pacing the streets with a bag of cat treats.

C   She comes home when she's ready, hungry or both.

D   If she got out and got lost, you'd easily find her by her mewling.

The Results

The Moocher

NEUROTIC & AGREEABLE

There's nothing this cat loves more than basking in the afternoon sunshine. The only thing that makes this even better is if you share it with him. Days spent in the garden together are a thing of joy and he'll happily lend a paw with a few horticultural tips while keeping the local wildlife in order. He likes to know where you are and he'll return the favour by never wandering too far. While his territory is limited, he'll protect it with his life. Woe betide any philandering felines on his turf! With humans he veers on the anxious side. A gentle character, he'll love chasing butterflies, but is rarely successful. The prize is in the chase not the catch. Should you be occupied indoors, he'll make his presence felt with regular visits to check you're still there and in one piece. Petting, pawing and lots of cuddles make this puss the Prince of Fuss.

Moggy On The Move

The Pioneer

EXTROVERTED & AGREEABLE

The Pioneer lives to explore. She likes to know what's in the immediate area and has a small radius but can be tempted further afield should her interest be piqued. Fun-loving and confident without being domineering, she'll avoid altercations wherever she can, but if push comes to shove her inner tiger emerges. Speed is her superpower and she'll run like the wind when faced with unknown felines and humans. With a nose for mischief, this kitty can squeeze into the most unlikely places should the opportunity arise. Play is important to her and every moment has the potential for greatness. While she likes to run free, she also appreciates home time and understands routine. There's balance in all things for this puss, so be sure to give her the space she needs and the option to stray or stay.

Moggy On The Move

The Wanderer

DOMINANT & IMPULSIVE

This feline has itchy feet. He longs for the great outdoors, and nothing and no one stands in his way. Life (and that means all nine of them) is for living, and he'll certainly get his money's worth. A born risk taker, this kitty pushes his luck, and is likely to have a few war wounds before his time is up. Fortunate, then, that he's not bothered about appearance. A few scars and grazes add to his charm. Bold and impulsive, he's not afraid to assert himself, particularly if he's not getting his own way. That said, he can also be super-relaxed, as long as you allow him to do his own thing. The Wanderer has a large territory which extends to most of the neighbourhood. He is King of the Road, and, as one of his subjects, he'll bless you with his company, now and again.

Moggy On The Move

The Homebody

EXTROVERTED & AGREEABLE

Humans and cats alike might find the behaviour of this lovely puss a tad strange, but far from being perverse she knows what makes her happy. Security is key. She treasures her indoor realm and while you might be forgiven for thinking you share the space, the reality is it's all hers. If you haven't already noticed her encroaching on all your possessions, then you soon will. From inside your favourite handbag to lazing in the bath, there's not a part of your home that she doesn't own, and should you ever think of going away, don't be surprised if you find her stashed in your suitcase. She puts the 'L' into loving, and you are her world, but the feeling is reciprocated. From spoiling her with her favourite foodie treats to devoting a huge part of your day to her, it's no wonder she never wants to venture forth. This self-assured puss has you in her paws for life.

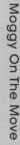

Moggy On The Move

117

The Feline Five
Score Page

It really is impossible to perfectly 'cat'egorize your cats, but we can try and identify key traits from the Feline Five (see page 9). Cats can sometimes display elements of all five factors, depending on their mood or circumstances, while others will fall heavily into one or two categories. It's a handy starting point for those curious about their cat's true nature.

Below are the five factors featured in the profiles at the end of the quizzes. Here you can leave a tick or a mark each time your cat matches to a trait, and keep score to discover which characteristics are most dominant in your cat:

1. Neuroticism
.... **Total:** ....

2. Extroversion
.... **Total:** ....

3. Dominance
.... **Total:** ....

4. Impulsiveness
.... **Total:** ....

5. Agreeableness
.... **Total:** ....

Conclusion

Each quiz is designed with different areas of your cat's life and personality in mind, and along with behaviours and quirks there's a hefty dose of humour too, because at the end of the day our cats bring so much laughter and warmth to the world.

Remember, this is just the beginning. The insight you get from taking the tests will you help you understand what makes your cat tick. Once you know this, you'll be able to help your furry friend live its best life by making any necessary tweaks and changes. From turning your home into an interactive play hub to making sure you give kitty just enough attention and dividing your time equally, if you're lucky to be living in a multi-cat household.

Whatever it is your cat needs to help it find its purr, you'll have a deeper understanding, and by taking the tests regularly you'll be able to stay clued up to its whims and wants. As any cat lover will agree, it takes a lifetime to get to know your feline, and you may never truly understand it, but you will have lots of fun trying.

Discover
More

What's Breed Got To Do With It?

Thinking of getting a new cat, and want to suss out how they'll fit into the family? Or now that you've completed the quizzes, are you simply intrigued as to whether your kitty is typical or a true one-off? Typically, different breeds have different characteristics, which can provide clues as to what makes them tick. Some breeds need more love, while others appear stand-offish, but what they lack in snuggles they make up for in style and street smarts.

Over the following pages, we've picked out some of the most common cat breeds, and shared which profiles might be a match. That being said, breed can only be a starting point. Cats are like humans. They're unique, individual and have their own quirks.

American or British Shorthair

This pleasant puss is playful and also happy spending time alone. Sociable and affectionate with family members, the Shorthair is fiercely loyal to its feline and human friends.

**Suggested Profiles: The Maverick (page 80);
The Charmer (page 103)**

Abyssinian

The athletic Abyssinian loves to climb trees, explore and have adventures. This curious kitty is quiet natured but forms strong emotional bonds with its human family.

**Suggested Profiles: The Chameleon (page 67);
The Pioneer (page 115)**

Bengal

The chatty Bengal loves family life and mixes well with children and other animals. Intelligent, loving and full of fun, this cat has big heart and plenty of character.

**Suggested Profiles: The Genius (page 43);
The Bare-Faced Beauty (page 56)**

Burmese

Known as the 'dog cat', because of its loyalty to its owners, the Burmese is extremely loving and enjoys lots of attention. This is a breed that loves to observe and watch the world go by.

**Suggested Profiles: King of Chill (page 31);
The Sheriff (page 91)**

Discover More

123

Cornish Rex

Some might say the Rex is demanding, but this cat just likes to be close to its human. Highly intelligent, and playful, the Cornish Rex is also a chatterbox, and can be vocal when it wants attention.

Suggested Profiles: The Boss (page 54); The Comedian (page 93)

Maine Coone

These gentle giants are sweet tempered and loving. They can be quite goofy and do enjoy lots of playtime. They have a curious nature, and get along with other animals and humans.

Suggested Profiles: Best Buddy (page 21); The Dude (page 66)

Persian

Gentle and quiet, the Persian cat likes a home that is calm. This puss appears regal, but is quite easy-going in most situations, just keep them away from boisterous environments.

Suggested Profiles: The Soft Touch (page 45); The Poser (page 69)

Ragdoll

One of the most laid-back breeds, this sweet-natured puss is calm, sociable and enjoys lots of cuddles. The perfect cat to blend into a family life and mix with other felines.

Suggested Profiles: The Baby (page 18); The Moocher (page 114)

Discover More

Russian Blue

Less clingy than some breeds, Russian Blues tend
to be shy at first, but once they feel comfortable,
they're extremely loving and also highly intelligent.

**Suggested Profiles: Cool Kitty (page 30);
Coy Cat (page 33)**

Siamese

Intelligent, resourceful and sometimes feisty, Siamese kitties
don't like to be left alone for long periods. They enjoy lots
of play and interaction and love nothing more than a long
conversation with their human. Highly athletic, they will
delight in climbing up curtains.

**Suggested Profiles: Artful Dodger (page 32);
The Intellectual (page 105)**

Further Reading On Cat Care, Wellbeing And Behaviour

Catherine Davidson, *Why Does My Cat Do That? Answers to the 50 Questions Cat Lovers Ask*, Ivy Press (2014)

Jackson Galaxy, *Total Cat Mojo: The Ultimate Guide to Life with Your Cat*, Tarcherperigee (2017)

Dr Yuki Hattori, *What Cats Want: An Illustrated Guide for Truly Understanding Your Cat*, Bloomsbury Publishing (2020)

Pippa Mattinson and Lucy Easton, *The Happy Cat Handbook*, Ebury Press (2019)

Amy Shojai, *Cat Life: Celebrating the History, Culture & Love of the Cat*, Furry Muse Publications (2019)

cats.org.uk/help-and-advice
The one-stop shop from Cats Protection, which provides advice on all aspects of owning and caring for your cat.

icatcare.org
The ultimate resource for cat care with an A–Z guide on health conditions.

thecatgallery.co.uk
Quality gifts for cats, and those who love them.

thecatsite.com
A comprehensive site, with forums on cat behaviour, health problems and living with your cat.

yourcat.co.uk
The website of the popular magazine, which has interesting features on cat behaviour, training your cat and top tips on cat care.

About The Author

Alison Davies has over 20 years experience of living with numerous cats and has been writing about them for many years too. She writes for a wide selection of magazines and has penned books on a variety of topics including animals, astrology and self-help. Her cat credentials include the books *Be More Cat*, *Crazy Cat Lady* and *Cattitude Journal*, as well as writing for *Take a Break Pets*.

About The Illustrator

Alissa Levy of @LevysFriends is originally from Kiev, Ukraine, but now lives and works in Germany. Her work centres around humans, their pets and their wonderful and ridiculous relationships.

First published in 2021 by White Lion Publishing,
an imprint of The Quarto Group.
The Old Brewery, 6 Blundell Street
London, N7 9BH,
United Kingdom
T (0)20 7700 6700
www.QuartoKnows.com

A catalogue record for this book is available
from the British Library.

ISBN 978 0 7112 6300 0
Ebook ISBN 978 0 7112 6301 7

10 9 8 7 6 5 4 3 2 1

Publisher	Jessica Axe
Commissioning Editor	Zara Anvari
Senior Editor	Laura Bulbeck
Senior Designer	Isabel Eeles
Designer	Maisy Ruffels
Cat Expert Review	David Alderton

Printed in China

MIX
Paper from
responsible sources
FSC® C016973